How We Use Plants

How We Use Plants for
Making Everyday Things

Sally Morgan

PowerKiDS press™

New York

Published in 2009 by The Rosen Publishing Group Inc.
29 East 21st Street, New York, NY 10010

First Edition

Editor: Camilla Lloyd
Designer: Matthew Lilly
Picture Researcher: Sally Morgan

Picture Acknowledgements: The author and publisher would
like to thank the following for allowing their pictures to be
reproduced in this publication: Cover: Ecoscene.
Ecoscene: 1, 4, 5, 6, 7, 8, 9, 10, 11, 12, 13, 14, 15, 16, 17,
18, 19, 20, 21, 22, 23, 24 (both), 25, 26 (all), 28.

With special thanks to Ecoscene.

Library of Congress Cataloging-in-Publication Data

Morgan, Sally.
  How we use plants to make everyday things / Sally
Morgan.
     p. cm. — (How we use plants)
  Includes index.
  ISBN 978-1-4042-4424-5 (library binding)
  ISBN 978-1-4358-2614-4 (paperback)
  ISBN 978-1-4358-2628-1 (6-pack)
  1. Handicraft—Juvenile literature. 2. Plant products—
Juvenile literature. 3. Plants—Juvenile literature. I. Title.
  TT160.M635 2008
  745.5—dc22

                              2007041069

Manufactured in China

Contents

Plants for making things

Plants are important because they give us foods, such as bread, rice, potatoes, fruits, and vegetables. They also have many other uses. Look around your home and you will see many objects made from plants.

The bark of the cork oak tree is stripped off and used to make corks and mats.

People have used plants to make things for thousands of years. **Wood** comes from trees and is one of the world's most useful plant materials. It is used to make buildings, boats, furniture, tools, and paper.

This ship is made from wood and the sails are made from canvas.

Other useful plants include the cotton plant. This produces a **fiber** that is used to make cotton **fabric**. Canvas is another useful material. It is made from the fibers of the hemp plant.

Trees for wood

Wood is an incredibly strong material. It is tough and lasts a long time. It supports the trunk of the tree and allows the tree to grow.

The annual rings are seen at the end of this cut tree near the Cambrian Mountains in South Wales.

There are two main types of trees. Broad-leaved trees, such as the oak and beech tree, have wide, flat **leaves**. They drop their leaves in the fall. **Conifers** have needlelike leaves, such as the pine and spruce tree. Most conifers keep their leaves all year round.

Did You Know?

Each year, a tree produces a new layer of wood and the trunk gets larger. You can see these layers, called annual rings, by looking at a cut end of a tree trunk. Each ring represents one year of the tree's life, and so tells you the age of the tree.

Hundred of logs have been stacked and are ready to be cut up into planks.

We collect wood by cutting down trees. Some fast-growing trees are planted as **crops** that can be **harvested** for wood after growing for about 30 or 40 years.

Making furniture

There are many types of wood used to make furniture. They differ in color, hardness, and how they look. Teak, mahogany, and oak are **hardwoods** and are among the strongest woods. Conifer trees, such as the pine, grow faster than hardwoods but their wood is softer. They are called **softwoods**. Softwoods are not so good for making furniture, because the wood is easily damaged.

Hardwoods, such as mahogany and oak, are best for carving. This carved door is in Morocco.

Did You Know?

Balsa is one of the lightest woods. It is perfect for making model boats and planes. The heaviest wood is ironwood, it can be used for outdoor furniture.

- Look around your home for doors and furniture made from wood. The most common woods that will be in your home are oak and pine. Look closely at the wood. Can you see the grain?

This is a close-up of a piece of mahogany wood. The pattern of lines that you see is called the grain.

Shaping wood

Wood can be used to make all kinds of objects. It is a hard material and can be carved. The carving is done with a cutting tool that has a sharp edge like a knife. Often, carpenters draw the shapes they want on the wood and then they start carving. Gradually, they remove the wood until the right shape is formed. Wood for objects, such as furniture, doors, and boats, can also be **manufactured** by machines in factories.

This decorative strip of wood has been made from carved pieces of yew wood.

Did You Know?

Marquetry involves sticking small pieces of thin wood onto a surface to make a pattern. Different-colored woods are used to make an interesting picture. Jewelry boxes often have lids that have been made using marquetry.

In the past, people made simple boats from logs. They carved the shape first, then hollowed out a place to sit. Wood is still a popular material for making boats.

This boat is made from wood. The carpenter shapes some of the pieces of wood by hand to make the hull (the body of the ship).

Plants for weaving

Many plants have long, flexible **stems**, which can be harvested and used for weaving. Weaving means threading the stems together to create a single object, such as a basket, bag, piece of furniture, or sculpture.

Did You Know?

Many woven baskets are described as wicker baskets. The word wicker refers to an object that is made up of hard plant fibers that are woven together.

Willow grows throughout the summer and then the stems are cut down to the ground in the winter. The stems grow back the following year.

These weavers in Ghana in Africa are making pieces of woven furniture, using local plant materials.

Willow is a fast-growing plant with stems that can be harvested in the winter months. Each year, new stems form. The rattan is a climbing palm that grows in **tropical** rain forests. It is used to make woven furniture and mats. Other plants that can be used for weaving include grasses, rushes, reeds, hazel, bamboo, and some lilies.

Making paper

Paper is made from the wood of conifers and eucalyptus trees that are grown especially to make paper. When the trees are harvested, the logs are taken to a mill and chopped into tiny pieces. Then the pieces are mashed into a **pulp**.

Papyrus is a grass that can be used to make paper. Papyrus can grow over 16 feet (5 meters) tall. It grows near lakes and rivers.

The pulp is mixed with water and other things to form a thick paste. This is spread across a long belt where the water drains off. The pulp is flattened by rollers, dried, and wound into a roll of paper.

Inside a paper mill, the pulp is spread across a belt so that the water can drain off.

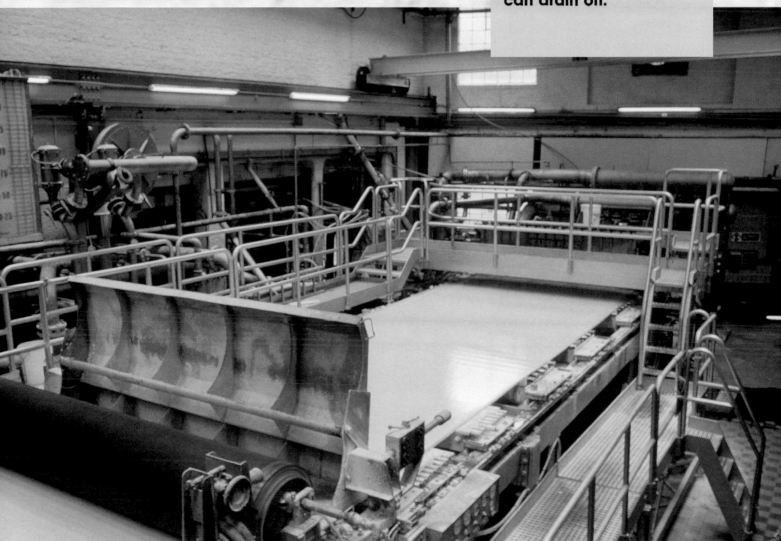

Trees are not the only plants that can make paper. Other plants, such as papyrus, reeds and rushes, palms, bananas, and rice, can all be used to make paper.

Resin

If you make a deep cut in the bark of a pine tree, a sticky substance oozes out. This is called **resin**. Resin is used in glue, printing ink, and chewing gum. It also has many other uses. It is a **raw ingredient** for paint, varnish, and turpentine. Turpentine is a liquid that is used to clean paint off of brushes.

Your Turn!

• The next time you're walking through a pine wood or passing some conifer trees, take a good look at the trunks. Can you spot any resin oozing out of the bark? Look for resin on cut stumps.

The bark of these conifer trees has been cut so that resin can be collected.

In some parts of Europe, there are large pine forests where the resin is **tapped**. The bark is cut and a small pot is placed under the cut to catch the dripping resin.

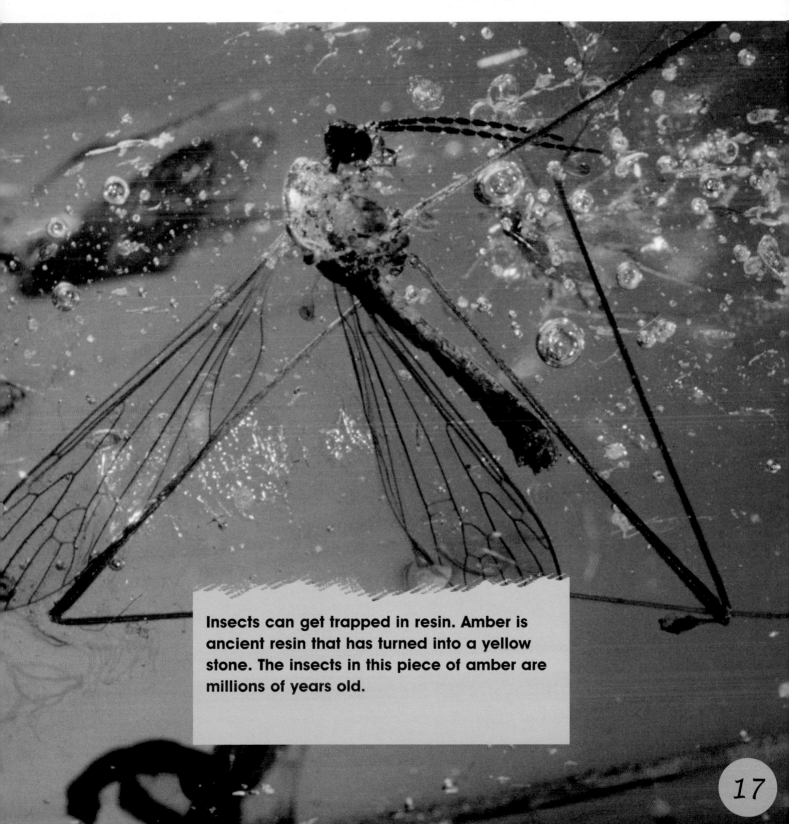

Insects can get trapped in resin. Amber is ancient resin that has turned into a yellow stone. The insects in this piece of amber are millions of years old.

Plant fibers

Have you ever tried to pull threads out of plant leaves or stems? These threads are fibers, which support and strengthen the plant. Fibers are also found in fruits and seeds.

These children in Bangladesh are collecting stems of jute. The stems are soaked in water before being used to make fabrics.

Your Turn!

- Take a look around your house. How many different types of plant fibers can you find?

Sisal and coconut fibers are tough and are ideal for making ropes, mats, and canvas.

Cotton is one of the most important plant fibers, but there are many other fibers. Flax is used to make linen, and jute is made into burlap. Burlap is a rough fabric. Hemp is used to make canvas fabric, too. It was widely used before cotton became popular. The seedpod of the kapok tree is full of fluffy, white threads that are used as a stuffing for pillows and cushions.

Making fabrics

Plant fibers have to be harvested and cleaned. Then they are made into threads and woven into a cloth.

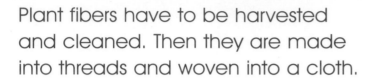

Did You Know?
Pieces of cotton cloth have been found in the Indus Valley in Pakistan. They date back to about 3000 B.C., and prove that the people of that time could spin and weave cotton.

Workers in Turkey pick the fluffy white seed heads of the cotton by hand.

The seeds of the cotton plant are surrounded by white fibers. Long fibers are used to make cotton cloth. The seed heads are taken out and cleaned by a process called ginning. This happens in a machine called a cotton gin. The cotton fibers are put in large bags and then sent to a cotton mill, where the fibers are spun into a thread. The threads are then woven into a cloth.

In this cotton factory in Zimbabwe, the cotton is spun into long threads.

Short, fuzzy fibers in the seed head are called **linters**. These are used to make cotton balls, felt, and soft paper.

Different fabrics

Our clothes are made from a variety of **natural** plant fibers. Cotton is one of the most common. Sometimes, cotton is mixed with a **synthetic** fiber, such as polyester, a fiber made from oil. Clothes made from polyester cotton are easier to care for, because there are fewer creases after washing. Linen, made from flax, is used to make summer clothes, because it helps people to stay cool.

The clothes on sale in this shop in England have been made from hemp.

Your Turn!

- Take a look at the washing instructions labels in your clothes. The instructions depend on the fabric. Can cotton and polyester cotton be washed at the same temperature?

The sail of this African boat is made from canvas.

Fabrics made from hemp are becoming more popular. Hemp is a fiber that was used to make the denim for the original Levi jeans, until it was replaced by cotton. Hemp is a hard-wearing fabric and is used to make canvas sails, as well as clothes and sandals.

Rubber

Rubber is an **elastic** material that can be stretched. When it is let go, it returns to its original shape. Rubber is used to make tires, waterproof boots, and waterproof fabrics.

The worker in this tire factory is checking new tires for any faults.

Latex oozes out of a fresh cut. The drips of latex from the bark are collected in a cup.

Rubber comes from the rubber tree, although nowadays rubber can be made **artificially**. When the bark of the tree is cut, a white **latex** oozes out. The latex is collected and made into sheets. These are sent to factories to be made into many different things.

Latex sheets are left to dry in a village in Burma.

Natural rubber becomes **brittle** when it gets cold, and sticky when it is hot. To stop this from happening, sulfur is added to the rubber at the factory. This is called **vulcanization**.

Bamboo

Bamboo is one of the most useful plants growing in Asia. Bamboo is a type of grass. It grows in a clump, with long, hollow stems and **lance-shaped leaves**. In addition to being the favorite food of the giant panda, it has many other uses.

Furniture: Bamboo can be used to make furniture and mats. It is a very popular wood in the Philippines.

Bamboo stems: The hollow stems are different widths. They are used in buildings and to make bridges.

Food: Leaves and young stems are used as an animal food. We can also eat bamboo shoots, and the flower seeds can be used as grain.

Cooking: You can cook rice in bamboo pots, and eat and drink from bamboo bowls and cups.

Make your own paper!

You can make recycled paper from waste paper. Ask an adult to help you. You will need about 30 sheets of used office paper, thumbtacks, a wooden frame about 12 in. wide by 8 in. high (30 cm x 20 cm)—an old picture frame would be ideal, two pieces of thin wood (plyboard) larger than the frame, a piece of old gauze curtain, washing bowl or tub that is large enough to take the frame, 6 kitchen cloths, a plastic bucket, and glass bottles.

Step 2

Tack the net to the frame with the thumbtacks, making sure it is stretched tightly. The next bit is very messy so it is best to work outside. Place a piece of plyboard on the ground and cover with a kitchen cloth.

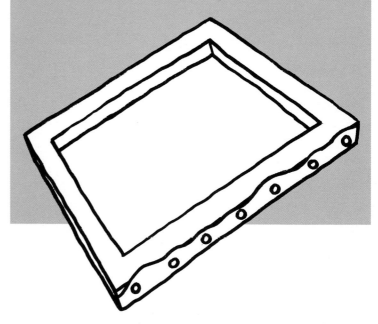

Step 1

Tear up the paper into tiny pieces and put in a bucket. Cover the pieces with water overnight. Using your hands, squeeze and stir the soggy paper until it looks a little bit like oatmeal.

Step 3

Place the frame in the bowl and pour some pulp into it. Spread the pulp around so that it forms a thin layer over the net. Lift the frame and let the water drain off.

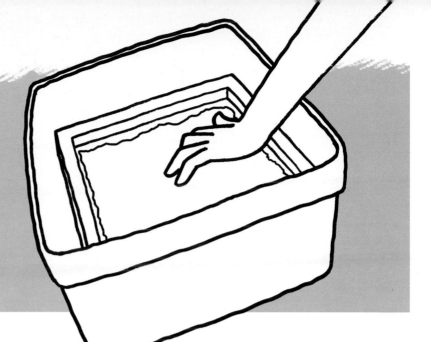

Step 4

Flip the frame over so that the paper is facing downward and then place it on the kitchen cloth. The pulp should drop onto the kitchen cloth. Place another kitchen cloth on top of the pulp. Repeat this process to produce 5 layers of pulp.

Step 5

Place the last kitchen cloth on the top, and cover with the second board. Put some heavy weights (such as full bottles) on top of the board to squeeze out all the water. Leave for several hours, then carefully remove the layers of paper on the kitchen cloths and allow them to dry in a warm place. When they are dry, you may need to iron them on a low setting to flatten. Ask an adult to help you.

Glossary

artificial not natural, made by people.

brittle easily broken.

conifer a type of tree with leaves that are shaped like needles.

crop a plant grown by people for a special use.

elastic stretchy. A material that can be stretched and will spring back into its original shape.

fabric cloth, material.

fiber a thread.

hardwood wood that comes from slow-growing trees.

harvested ripened crops that have been gathered from the fields.

lance-shaped leaves leaves that are longer than they are wide. They get narrower from the middle toward the tip.

latex a milky liquid produced by some plants like rubber.

leaf (pl leaves) part of a plant, a blade that is attached to the stem.

linters short, fuzzy fibers in the seed head of a cotton plant.

manufactured to manufacture objects means to make them with machines.

marquetry designs or pictures made of thin wood.

natural from nature, the environment around us.

pulp a mush.

raw ingredient something in its natural state that is added to other things.

resin a sticky substance made by certain plants such as pine trees.

softwood wood that comes from fast-growing trees.

stem part of a plant that supports the leaves.

synthetic artificial, made by people.

tapped drained.

tropical areas of the world that lie close to the Equator and that are hot all year round.

vulcanization when sulfur is added to rubber to stop it from breaking or melting.

wood a substance made by trees that makes up much of the tree trunk.

Further information

Books

Art from Fabric by Pam Robson and Gillian Chapman, Wayland, 2005

Art from Wood by Pam Robson and Gillian Chapman, Wayland, 2005

Science Files: Wood by Steve Parker, Heinemann Library, 2002

Trees to Paper by Inez Snyder, Children's Press, 2003

Wood and the Environment by Kathryn Whyman, Stargazer Books, 2004

Web Sites

Due to the changing nature of Internet links, PowerKids Press has developed an online list of Web sites related to the subject of this book. This site is regularly updated. Please use this link to access this list: www.powerkidslinks.com/plant/everyday

Question answers

P18 you may be able to find four, or even more. Common ones are cotton, linen, coconut, sisal

P22 cotton can be washed at high, even boiling temperatures, but polyester fibers should not be washed above 140 degrees Fahrenheit (°F)

Index